Down to EARTH

DAVID DAY

MICHAEL McPARTLAND

LION EDUCATIONAL
Oxford · Batavia · Sydney

Published by
Lion Publishing plc
Sandy Lane West, Oxford, England
ISBN 0 7459 1815 8
Albatross Books Pty Ltd
PO Box 320, Sutherland, NSW 2232, Australia
ISBN 0 7324 0268 9

First edition 1990

Design, graphics and illustrations
Simon Jenkins Associates

Photographs
Barnaby's Picture Library/Cyril Bernard, p.4 /
Gary W. Cralle, p.12 /H. Kanus, pp.15, 17, 23 /
Gil and Ann Loescher, p.25 /USIS, p.21;
Stephano Cagnoni/Church Urban Fund, p.31;
Greenpeace/Vennemann, p.16; Mansell
Collection, p.28

Printed in Yugoslavia

Contents

First impressions

It's a well-known fact. Empty houses attract vandals. In no time at all windows are smashed, flowerbeds dug up and graffiti sprayed all over the doors.

But if there are signs of life (for example, curtains at the windows, or even empty milk bottles on the doorstep) then vandalism is much less likely to start.

Both houses may be empty. Both are equally easy to vandalize. The big difference is that one is seen as a soft option. The other is seen as a risky business.

This book is about how we see the world we live in. It ranges from the personal (our bedroom, or the street where we live) to the global (planet Earth itself). As we will discover, how you see something affects the way you treat it.

Unit 1

A bit of peace and quiet

We might think that sound is sound. It's a part of our world and there's not much we can do about it. But sound is a very personal thing. More important than actual volume is how we feel about a sound. One person's music is another person's noise!

Noise affects people in different ways. Some people would rather listen to a road drill than an opera singer or a baby screeching!

Mike plays in a group which practises in the garage all Sunday afternoon. The sound they produce is fantastic. The volume is totally awesome. Birds' nests fall from trees, dogs hide under beds and the foundations of the house shake. Mike can't understand why his father keeps threatening to switch the electricity off at the mains.

Mike's father reckons that, unlike his son, he's a sensible sort of person. He plays in a sensible brass band. Which explains why he gets annoyed at the neighbours. He can't understand why they keep banging on the bedroom wall at three in the morning. He can hardly hear himself practising his trombone.

We all have different views on which sounds we regard as musical and which sounds we regard as noise. That is the problem.

Sound is a very personal thing

It's almost as if we have a built-in filter which takes out some sounds and lets others through. For example, most people will hear the sound of their own name in a crowded room, even if it's spoken only in a conversational tone. Yet the same people will become stone deaf if they're asked to do the washing up during the big film on TV.

The world is rarely quiet. Close your eyes for two minutes. Ask a friend to write down all the sounds which you hear. Were there more sounds than you were expecting? You probably noticed some sounds which you don't normally hear. It's a bit like the pressure of our clothes on our bodies. Normally we're not aware of them. The sensation is filtered out.

We are surrounded by sound

Some sounds we make ourselves. Other sounds are imposed on us by

Nice and nasty

On this chart, where would you place the following sounds?

1. the roar of a motor bike past your house
2. a baby at maximum volume
3. a jet plane overhead
4. a pop concert
5. the sea crashing on a beach
6. someone scratching their nails on a drainpipe
7. a car alarm going off at 3.00 a.m.

What other sounds would you put in each of these categories?

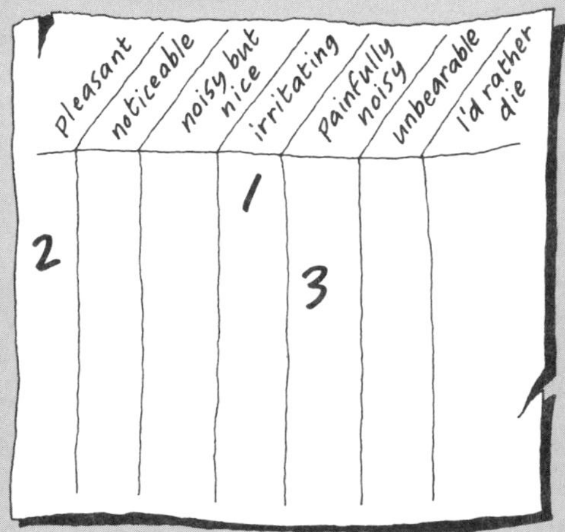

others. We may not like many of these sounds: thunder; a tap dripping; a teacher shouting. We call sounds which we don't like 'noise'. Other sounds, which we do like (waves breaking on the beach, wind in the trees, a child laughing) are music to our ears. Just like a favourite pop group.

Why do we dislike certain sounds?
We may dislike a sound because it is too loud, too powerful. The sound of a road drill, the sound of a jet plane overhead, or loud music, may irritate us. Scientists use a noisemeter, which measures the power of sound in decibels. As a rough guide, a sound below 40 decibels is rarely called noise, while a sound above 80/90 decibels is usually called noisy.

We may also dislike a sound because of its pitch. A high-pitched sound – the scream of a baby – may be more annoying than a low-pitched sound. Can you think of any examples?

Finally we may dislike a sound because it is irregular; it is unpredictable. The intermittent barking of a dog at night, or a door that slams every now and then in the wind – these can irritate you because they are not regular sounds.

So a loud, high-pitched, irregular sound is the worst noise of all. Can you think of some examples?

It has been proved that prolonged exposure to noise, sudden, unexpected noise, or loud noise can affect our health. It may cause high blood pressure, a rise in the pulse rate, shock, fatigue, loss of concentration and nervous irritability. This is particularly true of elderly people.

FOLLOW UP

1 Carry out a survey of the ten sounds your family most like, and the ten sounds they most dislike. You could conduct the same survey with the members of the class.

2 Where is the most peaceful place in your neighbourhood? What makes it peaceful? Where is the noisiest place? What makes it noisy?

3 Imagine you have been appointed the Noise Warden for your neighbourhood. How would you make it quieter and more peaceful? How would you persuade people not to create too much noise?

Unit 2

Neat and tidy

If you've ever been to a car-boot sale or a jumble sale, you'll know that what one person thinks is rubbish is someone else's 'find of the century'. There's a sculptor in the United States who makes works of art out of bits of metal that other people throw away. Once again, it all depends on how you look at it.

All societies produce waste material – things that nobody wants any more. Every day of the week we all put rubbish into the dustbin. Eventually most of it gets buried in the ground. Every year, the average family in the West throws away about one tonne of rubbish – the equivalent of two small cars! Can you imagine what your front room or your garden would look like after one year if you simply dumped all your rubbish in it?

Unfortunately, not all our waste material is put into bins, collected, and efficiently disposed of. A lot of waste is simply thrown into the street, the park, the school yard, the beach, the picnic site, the lay-by, the shopping mall, or the bus station... 600 tonnes of litter are removed each year from the New Forest. How many Mini cars does that represent?

Why do people drop litter?
We could try to think of a few reasons:

Rank the reasons in order of importance. What other reasons do you think people give for dropping litter?

The problem is that a lot of litter is not bio-degradable. This means that, unlike orange peel, an apple core or an uneaten sandwich, it will not disintegrate in the rain, the frost or the snow. It will stay there for ever, unless somebody picks it up.

If it is left where it is, it is not only unsightly but may also be dangerous. Broken glass injures children. Polythene bags suffocate animals. Small animals get trapped in bottles. An RSPCA officer recently found 77 small animals trapped in bottles in a single lay-by off the A5.

Why is there such a problem?
One reason is that we insist on putting everything into packages. Think of the things you buy in the shops. They are nearly all packaged. The drink has a can. The crisps have a packet. The shampoo has a bottle. Food is being packaged in more and more elaborate ways. Is it just for the sake of hygiene, or is it to make the food look more attractive?

Think of all the resources that go into packaging one item of packaged food. It costs nearly £10 million each day to package our goods. Somebody has said it is like eating oil! What do you think they meant?

The tragedy is that a lot of our litter could be re-cycled, but often isn't. The metal in the used can; the glass in the unwanted bottle; the paper in the discarded packet – all of them could be used again if they were recovered. Unfortunately, we live in a 'throw-away' society, and much of our litter is not recovered. In fact, the richer a society, the more it throws away. Each person in Los Angeles, on average, throws away the equivalent of 3 kilograms each day. In São Paulo, Brazil, it is about 0.5 kilograms.

What can we do about it?
Here is a list of possible solutions to the problem. Which do you think would be the most effective? Why?

- more litter bins in places where people meet
- higher fines for dropping litter
- returnable deposits on empty cans and bottles
- less packaging of food
- buying materials from people for re-cycling – make it profitable not to drop litter
- more anti-litter publicity

FOLLOW UP

1 Find a littered area near your house. Identify the types of litter, and make a chart which records the type of litter, the amount, and the people you feel may be responsible for it.

2 Devise a TV advert, a cartoon, a poster, a jingle or a car sticker aimed at trying to prevent people from dropping litter.

3 Here are five steps for reducing household rubbish. Rank them 1 to 5 in order, where 1 = most effective, 5 = least effective.

- Don't mix up your rubbish. Keep a separate bin for glass, tins, paper, so that they can be recycled.
- Apply the packaging test. Buy the product with the least amount of packaging. If it fails the packaging test (more than two layers) don't buy it.
- Buy in bulk. Buy a large bottle rather than six cans.
- Choose containers which are returnable.
- Choose natural packaging materials – paper and cardboard rather than plastic.

4 Produce a litter map of the school grounds. Where is there most litter? Mark it on the map. Where would you place a new litter bin? Justify your choice of a site.

I like the sound of breaking glass

WRECKED SHELTERS TO BE SCRAPPED!

Last year in Newcastle, over forty bus shelters had to be demolished because they had been vandalized. The windows were regularly smashed and graffiti was scrawled over the walls. The council had spent a total of £1,225 on one bus shelter in the previous twelve months. In the end, they became too expensive to maintain. As a result, if you wait for a bus in Newcastle, you will probably end up standing in the rain. Who cares? The vandals obviously do not!

What makes vandals do it?
Why do vandals destroy other people's property? Which of these comments make most sense to you?

Two boys once totally destroyed an abandoned car. They took it to pieces and smashed everything in sight. Finally they spent most of the afternoon throwing bricks at the wreckage that was left. One of them was asked how he felt at the end of what was called 'an orgy of mindless violence'. He said, 'Fantastic!'

That's one angle on vandalism. Have you ever vandalized anything? Can you say now why you did it? And how did you feel when you had finished?

Not a pretty sight
Unfortunately, there's another way of looking at this. Vandalism may make the vandal feel great, but it can have terrible results.

For a start, vandalism makes our environment look ugly. No one can pretend that broken bottles, smashed windows, damaged fences, torn-up trees and defaced walls look pretty. People lose pride in an area. They stop trying to keep it looking tidy and pleasant.

Vandalism also makes an area seem threatening. People begin to think it's a dangerous place to live in. Old

Graffiti

'Graffiti' is an Italian word. It means an inscription on a rock or a wall. It's a popular way of defacing a building. Legally, it counts as vandalism but, as we've already seen, everything depends on your perspective.

The person with the spray can obviously thinks it's OK. Perhaps he wants to declare a message to the world, or work out his hate against society, or tell everyone about the girl he loves, or make a joke. In the TV soap, *Neighbours*, Nick used to work out his artistic talents by spraying pop art pictures over a garage wall.

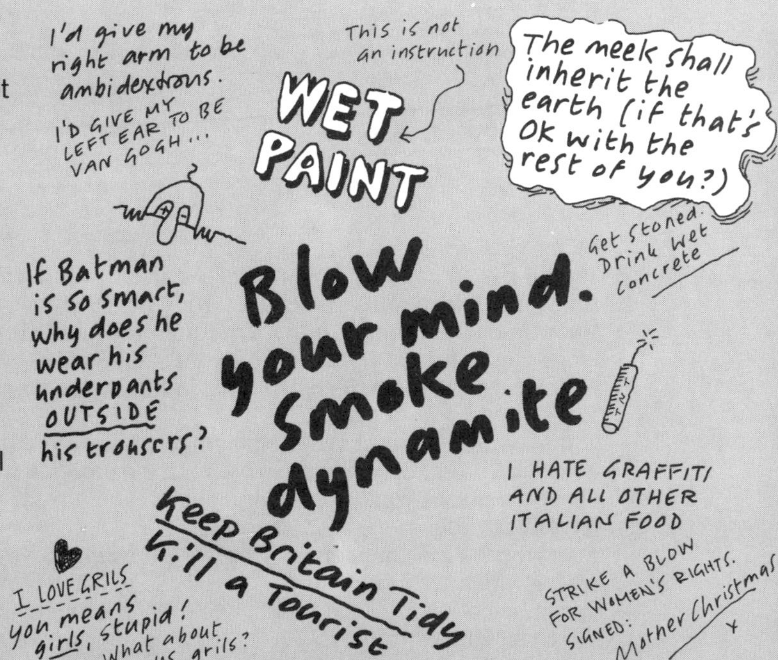

people in particular can get panicky if they see signs of violence and destruction around them. Waiting in a damaged bus shelter makes them fear for their own safety. Will they get damaged too?

And, of course, repairing the results of vandalism costs an unbelievable amount of money. Vandals sometimes think, 'So what? The council have got plenty. Let them sort it out.' But the more money that's spent on repairs, the less there is for new leisure centres, football pitches or coaching schemes. So who loses in the end?

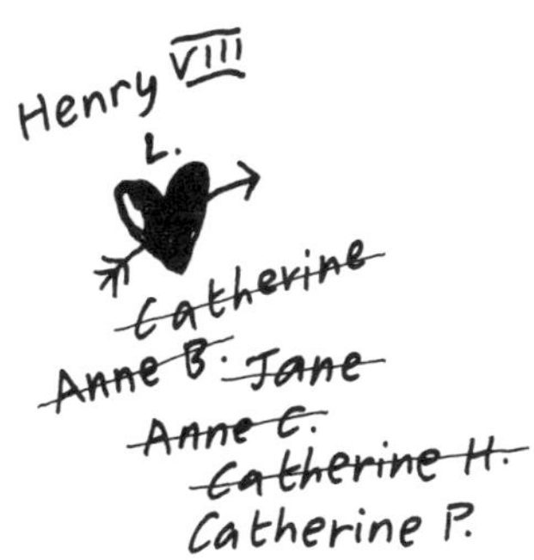

FOLLOW UP

1 Do you know anybody who has vandalised property? Find out from them why they did it. Imagine you are interviewing the vandal for local radio. Produce a radio script – or, with a tape recorder, do the actual interview.

2 Make a Vandal Survey of your neighbourhood. What kind of vandalism is there? Where is it? Can you produce a vandal map of the neighbourhood?

3 Perhaps some young people show little respect for other people's property because they don't really respect themselves. Produce a wanted poster of a local vandal. Describe him or her. Describe his or her personality. Describe the incident which occurred. How would you beat vandalism?

Unit 4

The world in my head

We all live in the world. But there's also a world that lives in us. My view of the world is probably different from yours. This is because what I value in the world (the things I think are important and significant) is different from what you value. My personality contains a whole range of beliefs, attitudes and values. And it affects the way I look at the world.

Our view of the world keeps changing over time. What do you remember about the places you have lived in and left? Close your eyes. What do you remember? These memories of the places which we have visited or lived in can be both happy and sad, satisfying and disturbing.

Here is the writer Laurie Lee remembering his childhood in the Cotswolds:

"Games in the moon. Games of pursuit and capture. Games that the night demanded. Best of all, Fox and Hounds – go where you like, and the whole of the valley to hunt through. Two chosen boys loped away through the trees and were immediately swallowed in shadow. We gave them five minutes, then set after them. They had churchyard, farmyard, barns, quarries and hilltops and woods to run to... Roundabout midnight we ran them to earth, exhausted under a haystack. Until then we had chased them through all the world, through jungles, swamps and tundras, across pampas plains and steppes of wheat and plateaux of shooting stars while hares made love in the silver grasses and the large hot moon climbed over us, raising tides in my head of night and summer that move there even yet."

When you have grown old what memories will you have of the places you have lived in?

Maps in your head

If you were asked to communicate your view of the world you live in, how would you choose to communicate it? You could write or talk about it, or you could choose to mime your view or do some drama.

However, you might decide to draw a map on which you represented your view of the world, putting in places which are really special to you. We all have maps in our minds. We have maps of our immediate world, our neighbourhood, of Britain, and even of the planet. These maps are called mental maps.

The images of the world which we carry about in our minds come in different ways. Some are formed from

our direct experiences – we visit somewhere, or go on holiday, or live there for a time. Some come from 'indirect experience' – we see a place on the television or read something in a comic or magazine. Then our different personalities take over and shape and change what we have experienced. It becomes a personal view. What we see and remember reflects who we are inside just as much as what actually exists outside.

Take a voyage of discovery into the world inside your head! Someone has called this the inscape. We can see seascapes, landscapes and townscapes, but the inscape remains hidden. It is the undiscovered country of the mind. But beware! If you draw a map of it, this secret world inside you will be revealed.

FOLLOW UP

1 Draw a map of your journey to school showing the features you pass on your way. Show it to your friend. Discuss what you have drawn. Compare your mental maps. Have you put the same landmarks on your map? If not, why not? Why are some places important to you but not to your friend?

2 We sometimes forget that other people and creatures have their own 'worlds'. What do they look like? Draw a mental map of your neighbourhood as if you were:

- a younger brother or sister
- grandparent
- a pet (dog or cat!)

3 Mental maps can be drawn at different scales. On this page is a map of the UK drawn by a Londoner. Don't take it too seriously. What is your mental map of the UK like? Try a similar exercise.

4 Imagine a visitor has arrived from outer space. It has just landed on Planet Earth. You are the first person it meets. It doesn't speak your language and you are forced to draw a map of the Earth to show what is happening. Your map needs to show the location of places and events. What does it look like?

A map of Britain, as drawn by a Londoner.

Unit 5

Into God's acre

The average graveyard contains a wealth of information on wildlife, plants, the people who used to live in the area, and so on...

It's not difficult to find a church with a graveyard. There's one in most towns and villages. The scene is often the same – headstones tipping to one side, or lying flat, half-covered in grass, weeds and nettles. It often looks neglected and unused, even though local people try hard to keep it tidy. Who ever would value such a place? Surely the only sensible thing would be to tear it up with a JCB?

Who values it?

This is where we came in. How you see something affects the way you treat it or value it. Your local churchyard is a valuable place if you look at it in the right way. It may look like a tip, but take a longer look.

■ For a start, **the local churchgoer obviously values it.** It is sacred ground. Human beings have always wanted to mark the final earthly resting place of relatives and ancestors. This place is special. It deserves to be respected by those who visit it.

Did you know? The area to the south of the church was reserved for most of the burials. This was the side where the sun shone at its brightest. The north of the church was reserved for the burial of strangers, criminals, suicides, the stillborn and the unbaptised. Most graves face east because that is the direction from which the sun rises – the place of God's throne.

■ **The local historian values it.** The churchyard is a mine of historical information. The headstones themselves provide information on the causes, time of death and occupations of local people.

Did you know? In the early days, the churchyard was the place for taking oaths, for settling disputes, for selling goods and for holding fairs.

■ **The local geographer values it.** The shape of the churchyard is interesting. The earliest graveyards were circular, but the Romans brought with them a preference for rectangular yards. Traditionally they were an acre in size (0.40 ha). That's why they were called 'God's Acre'. Many churchyards are located on land originally used for some kind of pagan ceremony, and therefore their sites were sacred even in pre-Christian times.

Did you know? The boundary wall of the churchyard was originally built to keep grazing animals out.

■ **The local geologist values it.** The headstones are made out of different types of rock: granite, sandstone, marble, or limestone or slate. These rocks are subjected to frost, acid rain and heat, which gradually wear away the headstones. This gives us a lot of evidence about the types and rates of weathering, and the degree of local air pollution.

Did you know? Headstones in city churchyards wear away faster than headstones in country churchyards. Why do you think this is?

■ **The local biologist values it.** All churchyards support a range of wildlife. There has been no crop-spraying or cultivation in the yard and so the natural habitats of plants and animals have been preserved. This means that you may find house martins by day and pipistrelle bats by night, swooping around the church tower. Mosses and lichens grow on the walls and headstones. Wood mice, voles and hedgehogs may inhabit the roots and holes of the trees.

Did you know? Many trees in churchyards have some religious significance. The yew tree is particularly popular in churchyards. It is supposed to have given shelter to the first Christian missionaries. The evergreen foliage is a symbol of everlasting life, and the red berries are a symbol of the blood of Christ.

■ **The local artist values it.** The headstones are inscribed with different kinds of lettering cut by stonemasons with great skill and artistry. The headstones often have signs and symbols carved on them. Urns with flames signify new life. Clasped hands symbolise farewell. And a dove stands for peace.

Did you know? Among the most common symbols carved on headstones are an anchor, a ship, ivy, an hour glass, weighing scales, an open book (the Bible), a snake with its tail in its mouth, and a ring. What do you think these symbols are supposed to signify?

FOLLOW UP

1 Plan a visit to a churchyard. When you first enter the churchyard what do you feel? Describe your feelings. How would you feel if you visited at night? Can you explain your feelings?

2 **A Churchyard Survey**. Make notes on the following...
- In what directions are the gravestones facing?
- Why are many gravestones tilting over?
- What is the most popular type of rock used for headstones?
- What is the most interesting epitaph?
- Identify three types of occupation of people buried in the yard.
- Discover the most unusual cause of death recorded on a headstone.
- What is the most popular type of sign or symbol on the headstones?

Unit 6

The world gets under the skin

We usually think of the world as being 'out there', separate from us, something we might bump into, but not something that can get inside. This section looks at the way the world 'does things to us'. The world out there has the power to produce all kinds of feelings and emotions inside us.

The power of nature

Take, for example, people's reactions to the power of nature.

■ Two small boys stand at the window watching a cloudburst. They're dancing up and down with sheer excitement. The rain is so heavy that the gutters will not take it. The road outside is like a river. The whole scene produces a kind of ecstasy.

■ For others, a thunderstorm or lightning will make them feel terrified and fascinated at the same time.

■ Sometimes a sunset over a calm sea, or dew on a cobweb, or sunlight shining through the branches of a tree seem so beautiful that they might almost belong to another world.

■ John MacKenzie, a keen walker, was on a climbing holiday in Scotland. He stopped by a mountain stream and spent some time just looking at the boulders that were sticking out of the water. He found himself thinking about the thousands of years that those stones had been lying there... perhaps millions of years. Long before life had begun on earth those stones had existed. Suddenly he felt very small and insignificant.

This is the fascinating thing about the world of nature. It has an incredible power to make us think about ourselves... To ask ourselves questions...Who am I? What am I doing here? Where's it all going?

Mysterious moments

Sometimes the effect of nature on human beings is even more strange. What do you make of this experience?

> I remember the maple bush at the corner of the sandy lane, with the sun shining through it, golden yellow, and I remember thinking of the burning bush. Oh it was beautiful. That I still see. And the sound of the water still I hear, running over the pebbles. And running through the long grass I remember – yes, this was something near what you might call mystical experience – the wind was blowing and there was this long grass. I was running through it and feeling a part of it. It was glorious, an absolutely glorious feeling.

This may seem a strange experience but it's more common than we think. Quite a lot of people have felt at one time or another that they were at one with the universe in some mysterious way. Usually these 'moments of illumination' only last a minute or two. People don't seem to be able to turn them on whenever they like. But nearly everyone feels afterwards that the experience was something special.

Earth symbols

This is not the only way nature acts on us. The world outside also provides us with a whole set of symbols to express

FOLLOW UP

1 What experiences of nature (climbing, sailing, walking, etc.) have you had which you remember as being 'special' in some way or other? Describe the experience. Why was it special?

2 You might like to think of other ways in which natural objects become powerful symbols. For example, what part do the following play in books, stories, films... ? The Mountain, the Cave, the Forest, the Tree, the Earth, Fire, Rivers. (Clue: the *Indiana Jones* films could be useful here...)

3 Carl Jung, a famous psychologist, claimed that our dreams are a way of expressing the anxieties which are deeply lodged in our minds. Our dreams often contain natural objects. If the following objects occurred in your dreams, what anxieties do you think they might represent?
- an active volcano
- a meandering river
- a waterfall
- a mountain cave
- a dark forest
- a wide plain.

These are all common natural objects in dreams.

what we are feeling. For example...

■ In some societies, **water** is a symbol of danger, evil or chaos. There are many stories of a great flood, when the orderly world was overwhelmed, 'everything fell apart', and it was 'the end of civilization'. In some of the psalms in the Bible, the writer talks about the waves going over his head. When we can't cope any more we sometimes say that we are 'going under'.

■ **The desert** has been a very powerful symbol for many people. The first Puritan settlers in America saw the wilderness as a 'pure' place. They could get away from the corruption and persecution of civilization, create a new society and get close to God.

It is also the place where you are absolutely alone with yourself, stripped of all your defences. In fact one order of monks regularly sends its members, one by one, to live alone for a time in the desert. The desert is a dry and barren waste, where you are confronted with your real, inner self.

The monks say that everyone needs to 'face the desert inside them and get the desert into them'. Then they will be able to cope with anything.

The desert island is a very popular symbol of the perfect place to get away from the problems of everyday life. Travel agents make sure that their brochures pick up this symbol when they are trying to sell holidays.

Greenwatch

Greenpeace protesters in a dinghy project a message for the world onto the side of the aircraft carrier Ark Royal. The ship carries nuclear weapons with 80 times the explosive power of the Hiroshima bomb.

Probably the biggest revolution in the last few years has been the way in which 'green issues' have come to the forefront of people's minds. Once, people thought these issues were just the hobby horse of a few loonies on the wacky fringe. Now the condition and future of the planet is on the agenda of all the major political parties. The activities of organizations like Greenpeace and Ark can make headline news.

The six commandments
There are six rules for good housekeeping on planet Earth:

1. **Be responsible** For each product you buy, ask: 'how is it produced?' and 'what effect will its disposal have on the environment?'
2. **Keep things local** Try to buy local products, and dispose of them locally.
3. **Keep things simple** Avoid over-packaged goods and over-elaborate technical gadgets. They are a waste of resources.
4. **Don't put all your eggs in one basket** Spread your choices in food, clothes and energy.
5. **Live non-violently** Avoid the violation of animals and land.
6. **Be moderate** Do you really need all the food you eat? All the heat to warm you? All those pairs of shoes?

Could you describe *A day in the life* of a person who tried to live according to these rules?

The green questionnaire

This section is designed to see how tuned in you are to green issues. What are you like at looking after the environment? Can you spot or sniff out an environmental hazard at a hundred yards? Have you got green ears and a green nose? Try answering the questions in the green questionnaire...

1. You hear your Dad and Mum debating about the front door. They want to replace it because your brother ran into it with his motor bike. If it were up to you would you...
a) choose something solid and long-lasting, made out of mahogany or teak?
b) go for a tasteful pine door?

2. You've had a hard day. You go up to the bathroom to relax. Now comes the moment of decision. Do you...
a) wash off the troubles of the day under a hot shower?
b) have a long, hot soak in the bath?

3. This fly has been buzzing around you for the last ten minutes. It must be your new deodorant that it finds so fascinating. You have a choice. Do you...
a) zap it with a well aimed blast from your handy aerosol?
b) chase it for five minutes with a rolled-up copy of *Flower Arranger's Weekly*?

4. You go for a quiet read on the loo. Do you know how much water each flush uses? Is it...
a) 1 gallon?
b) 2 gallons?
c) 10 gallons?

5. While you're up there, what do you think is the best colour for loo paper, ecologically speaking?
a) green
b) pink
c) uncoloured

6. The school caretaker is having a bonfire of garden rubbish. 'Nothing like wood smoke,' he says, breathing in deeply. 'Lovely healthy smell to it.' Your friend (clever clogs) says, 'I read in a magazine that it was a lot more harmful than smoking cigarettes.' Who's right?
a) the caretaker?
b) your friend?

7. If you had a choice of apples, which would you buy?
a) Cox's Orange Pippin
b) Granny Smith's
c) Golden Delicious

8. And what nuts would you buy?
a) walnuts?
b) peanuts?
c) brazil nuts?

9. There's nothing like a tasty packet of crisps. And these days they come in all kinds of flavours. Which would you choose...
a) hedgehog crisps?
b) buffalo flavoured?
c) prawn and treacle?

10. You seem to remember hearing that tropical rainforests were being cut down to allow more beef production. Your friend fancies going for a 'Big Mac'. You stand by your principles and say you don't want to support McDonalds. Who's right?

A bulldozer carves a trail of destruction through the rainforest.

NIMBY (Not In My Back Yard)

How would you react if any of these things happened to you?

- The city council decides to purchase a house in your street in order to create a refuge for battered wives.
- The local corner shop has to close down because fewer customers shop there.
- The local bus company applies for permission to operate a new bus route which passes along your street.
- A large retail company applies for planning permission to build an enormous hypermarket on an area of vacant land, five minutes' walk from your house.

For and against

How would you feel in the face of these developments?

In fact, we are all confronted by developments such as these. They are fairly common events. And our attitude towards them is determined by two things. How will they affect us? And how will they affect particular groups of people that we care about?

For example, the refuge will obviously benefit wives who need some temporary escape from their violent husbands. The old people will be denied the benefits of a shop within walking distance of their homes. People without cars will benefit from a local bus service. Large families might benefit from a hypermarket nearby which sells food at lower prices than average.

On the other hand, the refuge might affect the price of property in the street. The buses moving up and down the road will stop children playing outside. The closure of the local corner shop might mean less litter on the pavement. The hypermarket might lead to a huge increase in the amount of traffic in the neighbourhood.

So there is always a tension between the need to develop our world (more transport routes, shops, facilities) and the need to conserve what is good about our world.

The arguments between developers and conservationists are like a long-running game with no final whistle in sight. Sometimes the developers score a goal, sometimes the conservationists. In the middle is the referee (the government inspector or local planning officer), trying to ensure fair play.

The NIMBY Game

The following game is designed to help you get 'inside' the issues of development v. conservation.

- **The scene** Knorminster City: a World Heritage site. A city renowned for its beautiful medieval cathedral and castle, located within a deeply incised meander of the River Knor. It is a magnet for pilgrims and tourists.

- **The problem** About 2 km north-east of the centre of Knorminster is the Faversham Estate. The estate was bought by the county council over thirty years ago. At present it is the location of the county council offices, the police headquarters and the Knorminster Museum.

The remaining area of the estate – 248 acres – is occupied by woodland and rolling parkland. It overlooks the medieval core of the city. It is used by Knorminster people for recreation: walking, flying kites, picnicking... It has excellent views over the city.

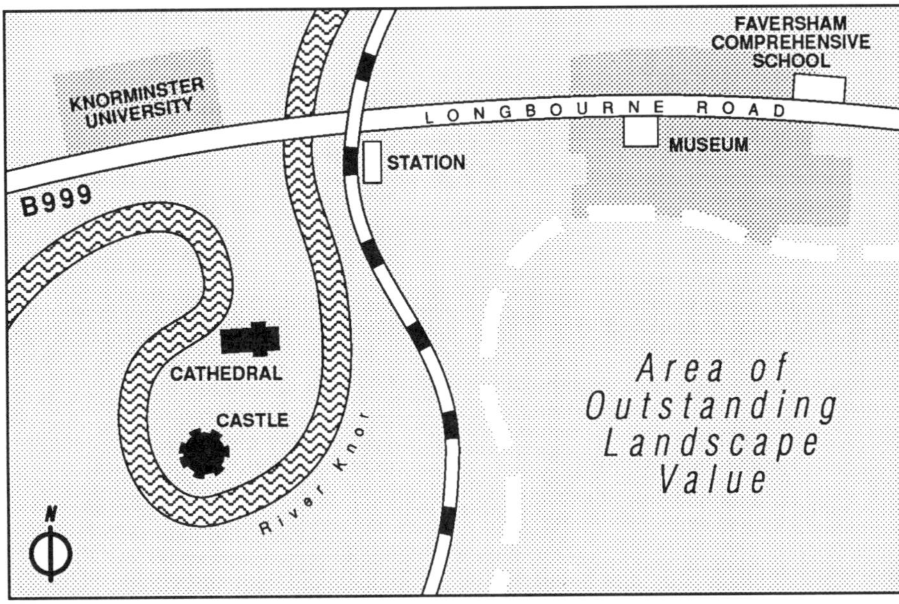

The battleground: Knorminster City.

The county council, which owns the land, wants to develop a science and business park (small offices) together with a hotel and housing development on this recreational land (see the map). The local conservationists are worried that the development will ruin a beautiful site within a beautiful city.

In order to try to resolve the issue between the conservationists and the developers, a Planning Enquiry is to be held.

■ **The enquiry** Divide the class into six groups. Each group will represent a particular interest at the enquiry:

1. The residents of Longbourne Road, Faversham Estate
2. The city council
3. The governors of Faversham Comprehensive School
4. The Directors of Curlew Hotels, a major hotel chain
5. The management consultants, Lawless and Morrison
6. The *Save Our City* action group

Your teacher plays the part of the government inspector – the referee.

■ **The groups** The concerns of each group are as follows...

1. Residents of Longbourne Road The development will lead to increased traffic, causing more noise and air pollution. New road-widening schemes will add to the disturbance. The new pub (envisaged to serve the new houses) will lead to excessive late-night noise. You think the quality of the area will decline.

2. City council The development will create many more jobs (4,000) for local school-leavers, who at present suffer from a lack of employment opportunities. The new hotels will stimulate tourism, bring more tourist money into the city, and create jobs in tourism. New executive housing will encourage companies to move into the area.

3. Governors of Faversham Comprehensive School The construction of a hotel in the estate will mean the loss of the only sports field near the school. The other school fields are several kilometres away in Saxton. A recent HMI report drew attention to inadequate sporting facilities at the school. The loss of this field would hinder the educational development of the pupils.

4. Directors of the Curlew Hotel Chain Tourism is developing in the city (cathedral and castle) and in the

region. A new 4-star hotel with conference facilities would benefit the company and the city. It is the ideal location for a hotel – close to the city centre, easy to get to, with excellent views of the city.

5. Management Consultants (Lawless and Morrison) Your task is to identify a site for the new computer facility of a large national company. A site in the south of England is out of the question because it would be too expensive, there is a shortage of skilled labour, and because of traffic congestion. You like the idea of Knorminster. It is an attractive medieval city. It supplies high-quality graduates from Knorminster University. There are good road and rail connections north and south, and to the estate. It is in an attractive setting, on an elevated site. High-quality housing would be in close proximity.

6. The 'Save Our City' Campaign The development would destroy a beautiful part of the city, with its woodland and open parkland. The parkland is used for recreation and the woodland is a habitat for a wide range of animals. In addition, the development will invade parts of the AGLV (Area of Great Landscape Value). This area was created by the council as a way of protecting the Green Belt of Knorminster from development. The AGLV in this area of Knorminster is known as the 'Green Wedge' since it is an area of land which follows the Knor and penetrates deep into the centre of the city.

The *Save Our City* action group claim that the development is against both the 'City and County Structure Plans' which were drawn up to protect this area of the city against future development. Finally, the development will also invade a conservation area linked to the railway.

■ **Running the enquiry** After each group has prepared their arguments (using the role cards provided) and picked spokespersons, you can hold the enquiry. This is how it works...

1. The government inspector chairs the enquiry.
2. The groups represent the views of the different interest groups described above.
3. Groups discuss their views in relation to the development and the roles they are assuming. A nominated secretary takes down their views.
4. One student acts as a spokesperson for the group, representing the group's views to the inspector, who questions the group. Cross-questioning from other groups is permitted.
5. New developments/decisions will be fed into the discussions at intervals chosen, at random, by the inspector. Groups respond to the new developments. It will often be necessary for a group to adjust its views as a result of the new information. (These surprise events are printed at the back of this book – do not look at them in advance!)
6. The planning enquiry ends. The inspector adjudicates.

■ **After the enquiry...**
Write a report which summarizes your views, together with the main arguments you used to support them. Produce a publicity poster for your group.

Gaia: the living planet

'We have probed the earth, excavated it, burned it, ripped things from it, buried things in it... That does not fit my definition of a good tenant. If we were here on a month-to-month basis, we would have been evicted long ago.'
Chief Justice of California

What do these things have in common?

■ Gary is watching late-night television after the central heating's gone off. Suddenly he shivers. It's getting cold. He gets up from his chair and puts on three bars of the electric fire. After half an hour he is too hot. So he turns the fire down to one.
■ Baljit is seven and is learning to ride a bike. Whenever the bike tilts to the side he falls off. After a while he learns to turn the front wheel into the direction of fall. At first he does this too sharply and he usually falls off. In the end he learns to turn to the wheel just enough to keep going.
■ Debbie likes to play darts. She aims for the treble twenty but goes too high. She over-compensates and puts her second dart below the mark. The third dart is OK and scores 60.

These examples all have a number of things in common. For a start, they're about feedback. Each situation is about someone who discovers that their first plan isn't working. They react to this information.

Next, they're about compensating – trying out a different plan to cope with the problem that has arisen.

They're also about discovering an ideal state. This is the whole point of the exercise – whether it's staying upright, keeping warm (but not too hot), or going for 180 in darts.

Finally, the situations aren't once and for all. The process of trying something out, finding that it doesn't work, and trying another tactic, is a continuing process. It keeps going on.

The Earth has a mind of its own
In the late 1960s, a scientist called Dr James Lovelock launched a new and exciting theory about the Earth. His revolutionary suggestion was that the Earth was able to react and respond to the physical and chemical environment. It was able to control

conditions on the surface of the planet. It was like Gary putting a pullover on or taking it off in order to keep his body temperature constant and comfortable.

The Earth seemed to organize things in order to make sure that life continued. Because it looked as if the Earth was alive, thinking, planning and responding, Lovelock called his theory *Gaia,* after the ancient name for the Earth goddess.

Hot and cold

It may help to try to follow just one of the things which led Lovelock to float this idea. The Earth spins in front of a very large electric fire (the Sun). The temperature is pretty near ideal for life on this planet, and has been for about 3.5 million years. But the Sun is not like an electric fire, because its output of heat isn't constant. In fact, its heat has been increasing steadily all through those 3.5 million years. It is now about 30 per cent hotter than it was at the beginning.

But if the Sun was that much cooler in the past, then for about 1.5 million years the Earth would have been frozen solid – much too cold to support life. Study of the rocks proves that this wasn't so. So what happened?

In some strange way, over all that time the temperature on the Earth's surface has never varied by more than a few degrees. It's as if the Earth has discovered ways of putting on a pullover until things warm up.

The greenhouse effect

Is the Earth warming up too much? About 20 km above our heads there is a blanket of gases. This blanket lets energy from the Sun pass through, but it also reflects some of the heat back into space. If the blanket trapped all the Sun's heat, reflecting none back, then the Earth would soon be too hot. At the moment, the balance between trapping and reflecting is about right.

Unfortunately it looks as if human beings are making the blanket thicker by the minute, increasing the heat trap. As more and more gases are released, so the temperature of the Earth will rise, perhaps to dangerous levels. As the temperature rises, ice at the north and south poles melts. What do you think will happen if large amounts of this ice melt?

FOLLOW UP

Look at these speech bubbles. Which of them fit in with the Gaia theory?

It doesn't matter what happens to the environment – the Earth will make sure life continues in one way or another. So we can go on dumping toxic waste!

We are the only species to be able to understand what is happening. We can help or hinder the system. This puts a responsibility on us to treat Earth with respect.

The Earth is a life goddess. In a mysterious way it really does think and plan ahead. We ought to live in harmony with it – this is the oldest religion of all.

If we foul up the environment then Gaia will eliminate the human species 'with no more pity than is shown by a nuclear missile.'

Gaia helps me understand the methods God uses to care for the Earth and keep life going. There's no life on Mars or Venus. The Earth is sacred...

Following the songline

Most of us can get quite sentimental about the place where we were born or where we lived for a long time. People feel proud to be a Londoner, a New Yorker, an African or Japanese. The part of the world they come from is home. We feel part of our home, and it is part of us. This section looks at a group of people who have a close relationship with their birthplace. The big difference is that for the Aborigines of Australia they are almost literally part of the land. And the land is almost literally a part of them.

At the heart of Australia, 2,000km south of the city of Darwin, is Uluru. The Europeans called it Ayers Rock. It is a huge dome of red sandstone which seems to glow – especially in the evening sunlight. Uluru is a sacred site of the Aboriginal people. The local Aborigines have lived around Uluru for over 10,000 years.

The Dreamtime

The Aboriginals believe that their land was created in the 'Dreamtime'. This was a time, long in the past, when groups of their ancestors walked across the land, creating and naming every hill, cave or dry creek bed. It is possible to tell a story from the Dreamtime about every feature of the landscape.

The adventures of the early ancestors were recorded in songs which describe how the land came into being. They are songs of creation. In fact, Uluru is at a point where the ancient tracks of several groups of ancestors crossed. These 'dreaming' tracks are called 'songlines'. For the people of the area, Uluru is a sacred place of the Dreamtime. They believe that they must hand on the songs which tell of its creation to their children and their children's children.

The Aboriginal people believe that places hold the spiritual power of their ancestors. Singing and dancing will release this power to serve their own needs. This means that, all across the land, each rock, salt pan, sand dune, cave or creek has its own story to tell and its own power. It must be protected at all costs.

The Aboriginal who goes 'walkabout' is making a sacred journey between sacred sites, treading in the footsteps of his ancestors, singing the songs of creation. The Aboriginals believe a land which is not sung about is a dead land. If the songs are not sung or are forgotten the land will die.

An Aboriginal father takes his children on walkabout with an imported camel...

The Wiyai Kutjara story

The Aboriginal Story of the Two Boys:

'Uluru was built during the Dreamtime by two boys who played in the mud after the rains. After the game they travelled south to Wiputu on the northern side of the Musgrave Ranges where they killed and cooked the euro. They then travelled north towards Atila (Mount Conner).

Sighting a baby wallaby, one boy threw his wooden club at the wallaby but missed. The club struck the ground and made a fresh water spring. The boys eventually died on the summit of Atila. Their bodies are preserved as boulders.'

The songs of the dreaming tracks also allow an Aboriginal to know exactly where he or she is located on the land. Each verse or musical phrase relates to a feature of the land. It is like a musical map reference.

Before and after the Europeans

Before the Europeans came to Australia, the Aboriginal people lived entirely by hunting and gathering for food.

In the 'greentime', after the rains, whole families moved out from their camp sites. They crossed the land in search of food and other resources. For the Aboriginal, movement meant survival.

When the Europeans came, everything changed. The Europeans were not used to moving. They settled down, and this had a dramatic impact on the Aboriginal way of life. The white settlers built their homesteads and huge ranches. They constructed railway lines across the ancient dreaming tracks, or roads to bring in the tourists. The water holes became polluted. The number of plant and animal species declined. The sacred sites were invaded.

In the early days, any Aboriginal who protested was treated harshly. The Aboriginal people drifted to the cattle stations or the towns, or they died of imported diseases.

In recent years, Australian governments have become more sensitive to the values of this unique way of life. They have tried to protect and preserve it. The rights of the Aboriginal people are slowly being recognised. Huge tracts of land are now being returned to them. In 1983, Aboriginal ownership of Uluru was finally granted by the Government. The sacred site was once again theirs to protect.

FOLLOW UP

1 The land provided the hunter-gatherers of Australia with all their needs. The industrialized nations rely on food producers. Keep a food diary for two days. Record what you eat. How much of it is natural, in that it comes straight from the land, without being processed and packaged?

2 The Aboriginal people know the name of every plant and tree in their area. Do you? Carry out a survey of the area near the school and identify the types of trees and the plants on the wasteland and verges. How many plants can you eat? Could you survive on the plants in your neighbourhood?

3 There are prominent land and water features in your area: a hill, rock, stream or valley. Study its shape and invent stories as to how it might have come into existence.

Keeping the balance

We have already seen that the way you look at the world affects the way you live in it. If you think it's a rubbish dump, you will treat it as a rubbish dump. If you think it is a gift from the gods, you will be a bit more careful about returning it in good condition to the owners.

This section is about a very important idea which was first written about thousands of years ago. It has come back into the news within the last twenty years.

It's the idea of balance.

Yin versus yang

According to this view, the world is like a pair of scales where one pan is exactly equalled by the other. It's like balancing a spoon on the edge of a cup. It takes great care to get it right,

Chinese belief in the forces of yin and yang determines the site and construction of their buildings. This tea-house is in Shanghai.

Unit 11

Yin and yang

What is the difference between yin and yang?

■ **Yin** The Chinese see yin in such things as: tranquillity, being passive, anything that is cold, dark, black, receptive or below. They see yin in the earth, in winter, the north, a valley, fertility and night; in lines and shapes that are soft, broken and gently curving.

■ **Yang** is the opposite. It is energy, being active, anything that is warm, bright, red, penetrating or above. Yang is heaven, summer, the south, a mountain, rain, sun and daytime; it is found in lines and shapes that are jagged, unbroken and harsh.

and the slightest breath of wind will tip it one way or the other.

We can illustrate this with a different picture. Imagine a ping-pong ball on a jet of water. The force of gravity is pulling the ball downwards. But, at the same time, the water is pushing it upwards. When the two forces are exactly right, the ball bobs around on top of the jet, held there by two opposing but more or less equal forces.

Something like this idea is at the heart of the ancient Chinese view of the world. From the beginning of the universe, two forces have been in opposition to each other. One is called yin and the other yang.

Everything that exists is the result of these two forces. But, as in the picture of the ping-pong ball, the two forces have to be in perfect balance. When they are, there is harmony. When either yin or yang gets too strong for the other, then disaster, chaos and destruction threaten.

The Chinese have pictured this idea in a sort of logo or symbol. The circle is made up of a dark shape which fits exactly into a light shape. Since they are exactly balanced and exactly fit into each other the result is a perfect circle. If one of the shapes happened to be too large or too small, the result would be less than perfection.

You can also see that the dark shape has a spot of light in it and that the light shape has a spot of dark. This is to show that there is no yin without some yang, and no yang without some yin.

Going with the current

What difference does this way of looking at the world make to people who live by it? Remember that yin-yang together are the stuff of which everything is constructed. They are the paint and canvas of the universe. So, it is said, you can see the constant struggle of yin-yang in the elements: earth, fire, water, wood, metal.

But the same balance of forces is going on inside the human body, in family life, the government of a state, a work of art, the landscape, or even in the bricks and mortar of a house.

If yin and yang are the invisible force fields which control the universe, then it is essential to live with them and not against them. The aim of life is harmony – not too little, not too much, but just right.

All the problems of humankind start when the perfect balance of yin-yang is disturbed. Human beings have the power to go with the power lines, or to fight against them. It's a bit like being a canoeist. Even in the roughest water the expert will paddle the canoe in such a way as to use the force of the current. The minute the canoeist fights the river, he or she risks capsizing the canoe.

It is easy to see why people regard this simple idea as the key to healthy living.

Building a house

It is especially important to get the yin-yang harmony right when you design anything that is going to affect the environment: a house, a garden, a road or a temple. Whatever you build might upset the delicate balance of the countryside.

The Chinese employ experts called geomancers in designing buildings. The geomancer works out the best spot on which to build, and the sort of building which will fit in most happily with the forces already at work in the land. This skill has become a complicated science, called Feng Shui.

Here are some examples of the rules of Feng Shui...

■ You need something tall and strong at the back of what you are building. A mountain is perfect. If you can't get that, then a tall building may do the job.

■ No building should ever be higher than the surrounding hills.

■ It's good if you can have an open space at the front of your house. In fact, a good site for building should be a bit like an arm chair, high at the back and low at the front.

■ If you are building a road, it is sensible to respect features like cliffs, big trees or outcrops of rock. Yin-yang lines flow through them.

■ Yang is often thought of as a dragon and yin as a white tiger. It is important not to wake the dragon. One of the best sites for building is between dragon and tiger. If you compare it to a person's arm, yang is like the forearm, and yin is like the upper arm. The best place to build would be at the elbow, where yin and yang come to a point.

Whether you think there is anything in these theories or not, they do mean that the Chinese look at the environment differently. It is already alive. Building a house without careful planning could wake the dragon, disturb the force lines and bring disaster. Putting it in the right place and thinking about the setting will bring peace and prosperity to the people who live there.

FOLLOW UP

1 Draw a map of a part of your neighbourhood. But draw it as if it were alive. Put in dragons and fantasy animals. Turn buildings, car parks and roads into mountains, forests and monsters. Try to find symbols and colours to suggest what you feel about the area. Where are the seas of tranquillity, the islands of mystery, the swamps of despair, the forests of danger, the maze where you feel lost, and the castles of security where you feel safe?

2 Draw a rectangle 16cms across by 8cms down. You have to divide this rectangle by drawing a vertical line from top to bottom. You can put this line anywhere – exactly in the middle, nearer to one edge or the other. It doesn't matter. All you have to do is put the line in the place which seems most satisfying to you. There is no right answer.

Now compare answers. Where is the most popular position for the line? Is it exactly in the middle? If not, why did most people put it where they did?

3 Try to find a building which has strong high support at the back, with an open space in front, where there is some yang on the left as you face it and yin on the right. If you can't find one in your area, then design and draw the perfect site for a house of your own.

4 Find (if you can) and sketch any development in your town where the planners have used something that was originally there and have made it a part of the finished design – instead of flattening it with a bulldozer!

5 Think of the house where you live. If you could redesign it and the immediate neighbourhood to suit the needs of you and your family, what would you do? Write a letter to the planning department describing your proposals.

Brother sun and sister moon

Many years ago there was a television play about a man who could hear nature. It was a peculiar play and in some ways a frightening one. It was as if he'd been given a sixth sense – the way dogs can hear sounds that are too high-pitched for the human ear. This man could hear flowers growing. He could understand the language of trees. Unfortunately, he could also hear the grass groaning when he walked on it, flowers yelling when he plucked them and the tree at the bottom of his garden screaming in agony when he started to saw off a branch.

Francis of Assisi preaches to the birds. Francis pioneered a different view of the world. He believed that all forms of life should be respected.

Every now and again someone does come along with a theory that nature can feel things in the way that human beings and animals can. They talk nicely to potted plants and play soft music to cacti. Whether this works or not is still an open question. But if you think the world around you has feelings, rights, and a heart, it makes a difference to the way you treat it.

Francis of Assisi

Francis lived at the turn of the thirteenth century (1182-1226). He came from Assisi in northern Italy. He was the son of a rich merchant, but he gave up his wealth to become poor, as Christ had been. In his own words, he married 'Lady Poverty'. He owned nothing and lived an absolutely basic existence, often in conditions of extreme hardship.

His religious faith gave him a strange way of looking at the world. This is captured in the famous song which he wrote: 'Brother Sun, sister Moon'. Normally, if you reckoned the sun was your brother, people would lock you away. With Francis it was different.

St Francis believed that everything in the universe had been created by God, and existed for him. If everything had been made by God, then every single thing you came across was sacred and had to be respected. You shouldn't despise other forms of life (and non-life). Humans were not the supreme rulers of the universe. They weren't top of the heap, king of the castle. Instead, they were one part of a big family which included the rest of creation. So it was not right to dominate, abuse or manipulate the rest of the created world. Everything was your brother or sister.

Francis insisted on carrying this viewpoint into his daily life. According to some of the stories about Francis...

- He removed a worm from the path in case someone trod on it.
- He preached a sermon on peace to 'my sisters the birds'.
- He negotiated with a wolf that was terrorizing the village of Gubbio and insisted that they shake hands (paws) on the deal.
- When he crossed a river on stepping stones, he did it with respect. He was treading on rocks and they reminded him of 'God who is called our Rock'.
- When someone offered him a fish he had just caught, Francis put 'brother Fish' back in the water. The fish refused to leave and swam alongside the boat until Francis ordered it to swim away.
- When he washed his hands, he picked a place where the washing water would not be trampled underfoot afterwards.

The canticle of the sun

At the end of his life, when Francis was desperately ill, the doctors decided that his 'treatment' would have to involve being burned across the side of his face. When he saw the red-hot iron he said, 'Brother Fire, deal gently with me for the love I have always had for you in the Lord.'

He put this view of the world into words in the famous Canticle (or 'little song') of the Sun. Here are a few of the verses:

'Be praised, my Lord, with all your creatures, especially master brother Sun, who brings day, and you give us light by him.

Be praised, my Lord, by sister Moon and the Stars. In heaven you have made them bright and sparkling and lovely.

Be praised, my Lord, through sister Water, who is very useful and humble and precious and pure.

Be praised, my Lord, through brother Fire... He is beautiful and joyful, vigorous and strong.

Be praised, my Lord, for sister Death...'

FOLLOW UP

1 Write part of a science fiction story about the day you woke up to find that you could hear the world of nature – whispering, groaning, singing, snoring, screaming, gossiping. Describe your experiences from the moment you get up to the point at which you arrive at school.

2 Do animals have personalities? What sort of characters would you give to a dog, cat, budgie, wolf, chicken? Imagine that your personality had to be housed in an animal's body. Which one would it be and why? Which animals would best suit the personalities of other members of your class?

3 Francis used to eat meat. Is this a contradiction? What do you think? Should people who say they respect nature be vegetarians?

Reclaiming the wilderness

Imagine the scene. A man dressed in a rough monk's habit and with a strange haircut is walking across desolate country, obviously looking for something. His companions follow him, a bit bewildered. The ground is uncultivated, a wasteland. It doesn't look as if it will be particularly good for farming. It is bleak, barren and infertile. There's an icy wind howling off the sea and black clouds are building up in the east. The group following the monk are depressed, muddy, hungry, tired and a little frightened. Local gossip says that the only things that live on the moor are wolves and escaped criminals.

Suddenly the monk stops. He looks round at the God-forsaken wilderness and smiles. 'Marvellous!' he says, 'This is it! Just the place! This is where we'll build it!'

The monk's name was Cedd. The date, some time around AD660. The place, in the far north of England, near Whitby. A king with the unfortunate name of Ethelwalk had given Cedd money to build a monastery. You would expect Cedd to find a lush spot where crops would grow and sheep and cattle could graze. Instead, he wandered about deliberately looking for the worst site he could find.

What is the inside story of this decision?

The lost paradise

To understand Cedd, we have to understand his way of looking at the world. In fact, he wasn't the only one to have this view. Down the centuries many monks had reacted in much the same way.

At the back of their minds was the story in the Bible of Adam and Eve.

In the Book of Genesis, Adam and Eve are put on Earth to live in a garden. The garden is called paradise. (In fact, paradise means garden.)

Everything is perfect at first. Adam and Eve are God's partners. Adam is responsible for the garden. He has to look after it. But this isn't a bad job, because everything is perfect. At the end of each day God comes to talk to Adam and Eve to see how they are getting on. And everything in the garden is lovely.

It doesn't last. Adam and Eve decide they will play at being God. They eat fruit from a forbidden tree. Disaster follows.

They are thrown out of the garden and forced to live in the world outside. Thorns grow up. Work becomes a desperate effort. They have to slave to get anywhere. What was a beautiful garden becomes a wilderness.

The story gives us a clue to the way the monks in Cedd's time saw the world. Here are some of the things they believed:

- This world is a wilderness. Left to itself it will become a disaster area.
- It's not meant to be like that. It's designed to be a garden (paradise) and one day it will be one again.
- It's good when you can take an especially bad bit of the world and turn it into paradise. It becomes a little symbol of what should be happening everywhere, and what will happen at the end of time.

This is why Cedd chose such a terrible spot.

God's partners

Not all monks were as extreme as Cedd. Some took the Adam and Eve story and emphasized the first part:

- The world is like the ingredients for a recipe. Everything you need is there, but human beings have to mix, stir and cook them.
- Human beings were put on earth to be God's partners – not his slaves.
- Their job is to take the world and make something good out of it. So they can change it and even improve it.
- Hard work is a good thing... as long as you are making a better world out of the raw materials God has given you.

Today's wilderness

Cedd built his monastery a long time ago, but his vision still lives. Many Christians have set up communities in a different sort of wilderness – in the middle of the squalor and decay which you often find in the centre of big cities, for example.

By supporting small projects to counteract unemployment, help single-parent families, counsel drug addicts and build good community relations, they are trying to turn the desert into a paradise, just as Cedd did.

In April 1988 the Church of England launched a nationwide appeal, the *Church Urban Fund*, designed to raise money so that 'cities may find healing and renewal and may glimpse the hope of the Eternal City, whose builder and maker is God.'

Florence Sykes from Newcastle had to leave her heavy factory job when her health failed. Along with many other unemployed people, she learnt a new range of skills at the 'Ucanduit' project, partly financed by the Church Urban Fund.

FOLLOW UP

1 In the United States, there is a sculptor who specializes in producing works of art out of garbage. Bring a number of bits of rubbish to school and try to create something useful or attractive or amusing out of them. You could try to create a wall-display of an abbey or monastery out of bits of material from home: pieces of cloth, wood, cardboard, etc.

2 Scientists have succeeded in breeding a new kind of mouse. It is called the Oncomouse. By altering the genetic code of ordinary white mice they have produced a mouse that is born with cancer cells already present in its body. It is guaranteed to die within ninety days. The director of the project intends to sell these mice to laboratories at £56 a time. Ordinary mice cost about 75p.

This project is changing the environment, just as the monks did. Do you think this kind of development is OK? How do you decide when a change or development has gone too far?

3 List three 'new creations': changes or inventions which you think have improved the world for all living creatures. Now list three which have made it worse.

Unit 7: Answers to green questionnaire

In each question, there's one answer which is right and earns you one mark. But, to be honest, this quiz is fairly light-hearted and the situation is often much more complicated. Many of the issues need to be discussed with your teacher.

1. b) is better. The destruction of the tropical rainforests is a major cause of environmental devastation. It is linked closely with the greenhouse effect. It's better to use wood which is sustainable (that is, it can be replaced).
2. a) gets the mark. In terms of wasting water, a bath takes about 2.5 times as much water as a shower. And a lot more energy is used in heating a bath.
3. b) is better for you because you get the exercise. It is better for the fly, because it will probably get away. The aerosol spray is an absolute no-no, if it emits CFCs. There are CFC-free sprays on the market, however, including two called *Buzzoff* and *Dragon* (for really big flies that breathe fire).
4. b) is closest. A standard flush is usually reckoned to be about 2.2 gallons.
5. c) is the best. Green or pink (or black, red and blue with orange spots) is more harmful to the environment. Coloured loo paper is less biodegradable than uncoloured. That means it doesn't decompose naturally in water as easily. The coloured dyes are also poisonous.
6. b) your friend is right. However nice it smells, bonfire smoke contains 70 parts per million of cancer-causing benzopyrenes. Cigarette smoke scores 0.2 parts per million. That doesn't mean that cigarette smoke is good for you. Just that bonfire smoke is very, very bad.
7. a) or b) score one mark. Golden Delicious are beginning to flood the market. This means less variety in our food, and more one-crop orchards, which are more vulnerable to attack by pests. This will result in a greater use of pesticides.
8. c) gets the mark. If the farmers can show a profit from the trees, there's a good reason for not chopping down more of Brazil's forests.
9. a) is the best, but it's a trick question. The *Green Consumer Guide* says, 'Hedgehog brand crisps contain no additives, are made from potatoes grown using organically-based fertilisers and contain only natural flavours. If you save and send in 20 tokens, Hedgehog Foods will make a donation in your name to British hedgehog conservation.' Would you want to eat b) or c) anyway?
10. your friend. You haven't quite got your facts right, although you were keeping your green eyes open. McDonalds have actually issued a statement which says, 'We do not, have not and will not purchase any beef from rainforest or recently deforested rainforest land.'

How did you get on?
7–10 marks and you're greener than the average Martian. The world is safe in your hands.
3–6 not bad. There's a definite greenish tinge working its way across your face. Keep going.
0–2 and you're a walking environmental hazard. Consuming, destroying, devastating, pillaging the planet.

Unit 8: Surprise events list

These events should be kept confidential to the teacher until revealed:

1. The council offers £25,000 to each of the Longbourne Road residents as a compensation for the increase in traffic noise and pollution in the vicinity of their houses.

2. An independent report claims that most of the 4,000 jobs created by the development would be highly-skilled and could not be filled by local school leavers. The companies would have to recruit nationally for these positions.

3. The council has offered to upgrade the school's sporting facilities near Saxton by building new changing rooms and improving the quality of the playing surfaces. They plan to compensate the school financially for the loss of the playing field.

4. The hotel chain has offered to move its national headquarters to Knorminster as an inducement to the development of the estate. This will bring the city prestige and more quality jobs.

5. It has been discovered that areas of the estate were landscaped with materials containing some toxic waste. The consequences of this are, as yet, uncertain. An independent scientific report has been requested.

6. The national company has offered to construct a major theme park (with the hotel chain) on the edge of the city. This park (called *Anglo-Saxon England*) is intended to compensate for the loss of the recreational space in the estate.

7. The National Coal Board has announced that Knorminster will be the site for a new national museum on the history of coal mining, with conference and leisure facilities attached.

8. A report has claimed that a rare assembly of flora has been discovered on the estate.